Published by Creative Education and
Creative Paperbacks
P.O. Box 227, Mankato, Minnesota 56002
Creative Education and Creative Paperbacks
are imprints of The Creative Company
www.thecreativecompany.us

Design by The Design Lab
Production by Chelsey Luther
Art direction by Rita Marshall
Printed in the United States of America

Photographs by Alamy (All Canada Photos, David
Fleetham, Jeff Mondragon, Stephen Frink Collec-
tion, WaterFrame), Dreamstime (Greg Amptman,
Michael Wood, Lianquan Yu), Getty Images (Awak-
ening, James R. D. Scott), iStockphoto (ShaneGross,
NaluPhoto), National Geographic Creative (BRIAN J.
SKERRY)

Library of Congress Cataloging-in-Publication Data
Names: Riggs, Kate.
Title: Manatees / Kate Riggs.
Series: Amazing Animals.
Includes bibliographical references and index.
Summary: A basic exploration of the appearance,
behavior, and habitat of manatees, the aquatic
relatives of dugongs. Also included is a story from
folklore explaining why manatees are associated with
mermaids.
Identifiers: ISBN 978-1-60818-879-6 (hardcover)
/ ISBN 978-1-62832-495-2 (pbk) / ISBN 978-1-
56660-931-9 (eBook)

This title has been submitted for CIP processing under
LCCN 2017937490.

CCSS: RI.1.1, 2, 4, 5, 6, 7; RI.2.2, 5, 6, 7, 10;
RI.3.1, 5, 7, 8; RF.1.1, 3, 4; RF.2.3, 4

First Edition HC 9 8 7 6 5 4 3 2 1
First Edition PBK 9 8 7 6 5 4 3 2 1

AMAZING ANIMALS

MANATEES

BY KATE RIGGS

CREATIVE EDUCATION • CREATIVE PAPERBACKS

Curved flippers help manatees turn and roll over in water

Manatees live in warm waters. There are three **species**. West Indian manatees can be seen off the coast of Florida and in the Caribbean. Other manatees live in Africa and South America.

species a group of similar (or closely related) animals

The manatee's body is covered with whiskers. The short hairs help the animal feel for food and other things. A manatee has an upper lip that has two parts. Each part works like a finger to grip food.

The whiskers on manatees' snouts are extra sensitive

Manatees are large animals. Some people call them "sea cows." Many average about 1,200 pounds (544 kg) in weight and up to 13 feet (4 m) in length. Amazonian manatees are the smaller kind. They typically do not weigh more than 1,000 pounds (454 kg).

West Indian manatees can weigh up to 3,000 pounds (1,361 kg)

Water warmer than 68 °F (20 °C) is best for manatees. They swim using their tail and front flippers. Most manatees' flippers have fingernails. These dig into the sand to help a manatee "walk" underwater.

Despite their large size, manatees have little fat and are easily chilled

Manatees hold their breath. They search for water plants. They chew using six large cheek teeth.

Manatees eat 10 to 15 percent of their body weight daily

*Mother manatees lift
calves to the surface
to help them breathe*

A mother manatee usually has one **calf** at a time. The newborn weighs 60 to 70 pounds (27.2–31.8 kg). The calf swims with its mother. It eats plants and her milk for about two years.

calf a baby manatee

Manatees often gather in small groups. They look for food in the same places. They may play together. They rub faces or touch flippers.

A larger group of manatees is called an aggregation

Manatees spend six to eight hours looking for food. They sleep for 8 to 10 hours a day. A sleeping manatee can hold its breath for 20 minutes! But then it needs to breathe air.

Manatees typically hold their breath for three to five minutes

Some people swim with manatees in Florida. They float on the water. Manatees move around them. It can be fun to see these gentle giants up-close!

Slow-moving manatees swim about five miles (8 km) per hour

A Manatee Story

What do mermaids have to do with manatees? People in Portugal told a story about this. Long ago, a storm tossed a man off his ship. A mermaid saved him near Africa. He asked the mermaid to come back with him. She made herself a heavy coat, so she could swim in colder waters. But the man was not able to return for her. So she still swims along the African shore, as a manatee.

Read More

Marsh, Laura. *Manatees*. Washington, D.C.: National Geographic, 2014.

Pettiford, Rebecca. *Manatees*. Minneapolis: Bellwether Media, 2017.

Websites

National Geographic Kids: West Indian Manatee
http://kids.nationalgeographic.com/animals/west-indian-manatee/#west-indian -manatee-group.jpg
Learn more about West Indian manatees.

Save the Manatee Club: Get Manatee Materials
http://www.savethemanatee.org/manatee.materials.htm
This site has manatee facts and activity pages.

Note: Every effort has been made to ensure that the websites listed above are suitable for children, that they have educational value, and that they contain no inappropriate material. However, because of the nature of the Internet, it is impossible to guarantee that these sites will remain active indefinitely or that their contents will not be altered.

Index